Pennsylvania

BY ANN HEINRICHS

Content Adviser: Kathy Hale, State Library of Pennsylvania, Harrisburg, Pennsylvania

Reading Adviser: Dr. Linda D. Labbo, Department of Reading Education, College of Education, The University of Georgia

COMPASS POINT BOOKS • MINNEAPOLIS, MINNESOTA

Compass Point Books
3109 West 50th Street, #115
Minneapolis, MN 55410

Visit Compass Point Books on the Internet at *www.compasspointbooks.com*
or e-mail your request to *custserv@compasspointbooks.com*

On the cover: Gettysburg Battlefield

Photographs ©: PhotoDisc, cover, 1, 47; W. Cody/Corbis, 3, 8; TRIP/J. Isachsenn, 4; Topham
Picturepoint, 7, 12, 15, 16, 22, 24, 39, 41, 43 (top), 48 (top); TRIP/Viesti Collection, 10; Topham/Photri,
11, 45; Ann Ronan Picture Library, 13, 14, 42; Charles E. Rotkin/Corbis, 17, 20; Kevin Schafer/Corbis,
18; Lee Snider/Corbis, 19; Topham/ImageWorks, 23; Richard T. Nowitz/Corbis, 25; TRIP/J. Greenberg,
26, 28, 35, 36; Najlah Feanny/CORBIS SABA, 27; TRIP/M. Stevenson, 29; TRIP/T. Campbell, 30, 46;
Empics/Tony Marshall, 31; Empics/Steve Lipofsky, 32; Reuters NewMedia, Inc./Corbis, 33; Buddy
Mays/Corbis, 34; TRIP/J. Melhuish, 37; David Muench/Corbis, 40; Robesus, Inc, 43 (state flag); One
Mile Up, Inc., 43 (state seal); Kent & Donna Dannen, 44 (top & middle); Ingram Publishing, 44 (bottom).

Editors: E. Russell Primm, Emily J. Dolbear, and Catherine Neitge
Photo Researchers: Svetlana Zhurkina and Image Select International
Photo Selector: Linda S. Koutris
Designer/Page Production: The Design Lab/Jaime Martens
Cartographer: XNR Productions, Inc.

Library of Congress Cataloging-in-Publication Data
Heinrichs, Ann.
    Pennsylvania / by Ann Heinrichs.
        p. cm.— (This land is your land)
    Summary: Introduces the geography, history, government, people, culture, and attractions of
Pennsylvania.
    Includes bibliographical references and index.
    ISBN 0-7565-0320-5 (hardcover)
    1. Pennsylvania—Juvenile literature. [1. Pennsylvania.] I. Title. II. Series: Heinrichs, Ann. This land is
your land.
  F149.3.H46 2003
    974.8—dc21   2002010104

Table of Contents

NOTE: In this book, words that are defined in the glossary are in **bold** *the first time they appear in the text.*

▲ Steelworks near the Ohio River south of Pittsburgh

"All men are created equal," the speaker cried out. They have the right to "life, liberty, and the pursuit of happiness!" The crowds cheered wildly when they heard these exciting words.

This scene took place in Philadelphia, Pennsylvania, in 1776. It was the first public reading of the Declaration of Independence.

Pennsylvania has played a major role in the history of the United States. It was the second state to join the Union. The city of Philadelphia was the U.S. capital from 1790 to 1800. In the Civil War (1861–1865), the important Battle of Gettysburg took place in Pennsylvania.

Pennsylvania grew into an industrial giant. It supplied America with coal and steel. The state has also kept its natural beauty. Wild creatures still roam through its forest-covered mountains. Now let's explore Pennsylvania and discover its many wonders.

Pennsylvania lies near the East Coast of the United States. New Jersey is on its eastern edge. To the south is Maryland. New York lines the northern border. Pennsylvania's northwest corner faces Lake Erie, while West Virginia bends around Pennsylvania's southwest corner. Ohio lies to the west.

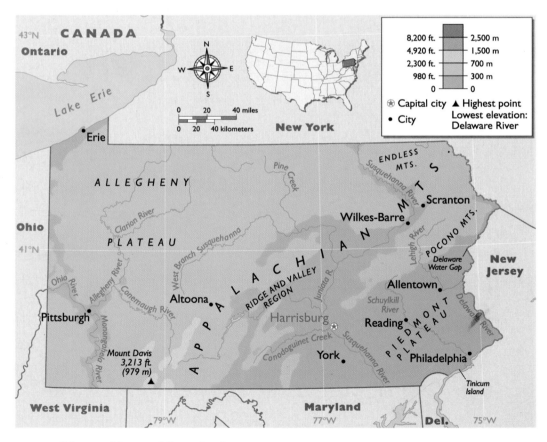

▲ **A topographic map of Pennsylvania**

▲ **The Allegheny and Monongahela Rivers join to form the Ohio River at Pittsburgh.**

Pennsylvania has a rolling landscape of hills and valleys. The Appalachian Mountains cover most of the state. They run almost all the way down the eastern United States.

The Appalachians have many different sections. One is the Allegheny **Plateau.** It covers north and west Pennsylvania, stretching across half the state. This land is high and rough. Rivers and streams cut narrow valleys through its flat-topped hills. At one point, the Allegheny and Monongahela Rivers meet. They join to form the Ohio River at Pittsburgh.

▲ Rocky hills and waterfalls make up the landscape of the Pennsylvania Appalachians.

One part of northwest Pennsylvania is not hilly at all, however. That part is the fertile plain near Lake Erie. On the lakeshore sits the port city of Erie.

The **Ridge** and Valley Region of the Appalachians lies just east of the Allegheny Plateau. This section has long strips of spiny ridges, or rocky hills. Deep valleys with rich soil lie between the ridges.

Rolling hills and plains cover southeast Pennsylvania. This region is called the Piedmont Plateau. Some of the state's best farmland is found here. Harrisburg, the state capital, is also on the Piedmont Plateau.

Forests cover more than half the state. These wooded lands shelter deer, woodchucks, foxes, bobcats, and rabbits. Pennsylvania's largest animals are elks, with their big, branching horns. Wild turkeys and ruffed grouse—the state bird—also live in the woodlands. Black bears roam through the mountains, and the rivers and streams are alive with trout and pike.

The Delaware River is Pennsylvania's most important river. It forms Pennsylvania's entire eastern border. One of its

▲ **Philadelphia is located along the Schuylkill River.**

tributaries is the Schuylkill River. The Schuylkill meets the Delaware south of Philadelphia, Pennsylvania's largest city.

The Susquehanna is another important river. It rises in New York to the north and runs through eastern Pennsylvania. The Susquehanna has many branches.

People in northwest Pennsylvania have very snowy winters. Northern Pennsylvania gets much colder than the southern part of the state. When summer comes, the southeast is the warmest part of the state. Many Pennsylvanians love autumn the best. That's when leaves turn beautiful colors across the hillsides.

▲ Autumn at the John Heinz National Wildlife Refuge at Tinicum

▲ **Henry Hudson sailing into the Delaware River Bay**

Many Native Americans once lived in Pennsylvania. The Delaware Indians lived in the Delaware River Valley. They called themselves Lenape, which means "genuine people." They raised beans, squash, tobacco, and maize, or corn. They made their homes of curved branches covered with bark or woven mats.

Henry Hudson was probably the first European in Pennsylvania. He sailed into Delaware River Bay in 1609. In 1643, settlers arrived from Sweden. Their little **colony,** New Sweden, was the first European settlement in Pennsylvania. In 1664, the English took over the region.

King Charles II of England let William Penn start a colony in 1681. It was named Pennsylvania, meaning "Penn's Woods," after William's father. Pennsylvania became one of Great Britain's thirteen colonies in North America.

▲ **William Penn traded with Native Americans.**

▲ **The signing of the Declaration of Independence in Philadelphia, as painted by John Trumbull**

Penn belonged to the Quaker religion, but he welcomed all religions in his colony. He founded Philadelphia, which means "city of brotherly love."

Over time, the **colonists** wanted their freedom. They formed the Continental Congress to decide what to do. The Congress first met in Philadelphia in 1774. The very next year, the Revolutionary War (1775–1783) began. In 1776, the Declaration of Independence was signed in Philadelphia. Benjamin Franklin was one of the signers for Pennsylvania.

At last, in 1783, the colonists won the war. Representatives met in Philadelphia again. They wrote a **constitution** describing how their government would work. As soon as a colony accepted the U.S. Constitution, it became a U.S. state. Delaware was the first colony to accept. Then, on December 12, 1787, Pennsylvania voted yes. It became the second state.

Great Britain was still a problem, though. Its ships continued to stop U.S. ships and take their sailors. Finally, Congress declared the War of 1812 (1812–1815). Commodore Oliver Hazard Perry sailed out from Lake Erie. He won a great victory in the Battle of Lake Erie.

▲ Commodore Perry won the Battle of Lake Erie against the British during the War of 1812.

In the 1850s, Northern and Southern states were splitting apart over the issue of slavery. Finally, their differences exploded into the Civil War. In 1863, one of the war's bloodiest battles took place in Gettysburg, Pennsylvania. Later that year, President Abraham Lincoln gave his famous Gettysburg Address there.

▲ The Battle of Gettysburg was one of the bloodiest of the Civil War.

▲ For decades, steelmaking has been an important part of Pennsylvania's economy.

Pennsylvania grew quickly after the war. Farms, coal mines, and steel factories produced tons of goods. By the early 1900s, Pennsylvania had many huge **industries.**

During World War II (1939–1945), Pennsylvania provided many war supplies. After the war, however, the state's businesses slowed down. State leaders worked hard to improve the **economy.**

Today, new industries such as **electronics** are growing fast. Millions of visitors are discovering Pennsylvania, too. They see why Pennsylvanians are proud of their state!

▲ *Phacops rana* **became the state fossil in 1988.**

Anyone can make a difference in their government—even
children! Some elementary school students in Pennsylvania
proved that. In science class, they were studying **fossils.** A
marine animal called *Phacops rana* lived in Pennsylvania
millions of years ago. The students thought it would make a
great state fossil. They wrote to their state lawmakers, and
the lawmakers agreed! In 1988, *Phacops rana* became
Pennsylvania's official state fossil.

Pennsylvania's lawmakers, as the name suggests, make the state's laws. Together, they make up the legislative branch of state government. That's one of Pennsylvania's three branches of government—legislative, executive, and judicial. The U.S. government has those same three branches.

The state's lawmakers serve in Pennsylvania's general assembly. It has two houses, or parts—a 50-member senate and a 203-member house of representatives.

▲ **The Pennsylvania capitol**

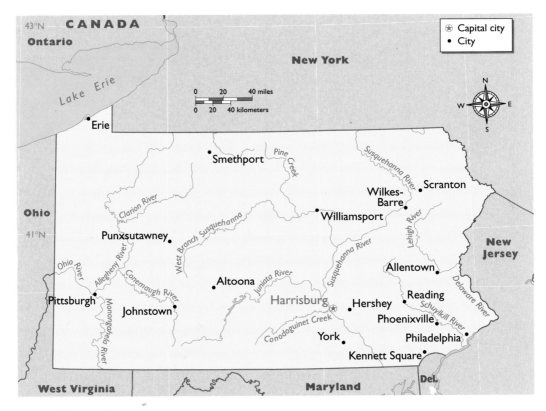

▲ A geopolitical map of Pennsylvania

The executive branch makes sure the state's laws are carried out. Pennsylvania's governor leads the executive branch. Voters choose a governor every four years. The governor also has a cabinet—a group of assistants. They give advice and help.

The judicial branch is made up of judges and courts. The judges decide whether someone has broken the law and how he or she should be punished. Pennsylvania's highest court is the state supreme court.

Pennsylvania is divided into sixty-seven counties. Most counties elect a three-member board of commissioners. Townships, cities, and boroughs have governments, too. Townships elect commissioners or supervisors. Most cities and boroughs elect a mayor and a city council.

Philadelphia is both a city and a county. Its mayor and council rule both the city and the county.

Pennsylvania's official name is the Commonwealth of Pennsylvania. A commonwealth is like a state. Its government is working for the good of all.

▲ The Pennsylvania countryside is dotted with small towns.

▲ **Millionaire Andrew Mellon donated money to build the National Gallery of Art.**

What would you do if you had millions of dollars? Pennsylvania's "captains of industry" had that choice in the late nineteenth and early twentieth centuries.

Andrew Mellon started the Aluminum Company of America (Alcoa). Then he used his money to help build the National Gallery of Art in Washington, D.C. Henry Clay Frick's company processed coke, a by-product of coal. Frick built hospitals, schools, and an art museum. Andrew Carnegie built a railroad, steel, and coal empire.

▲ A steel mill near Pittsburgh

Then he donated the money to build almost three thousand public libraries throughout the United States.

Coal, iron, and steel were once Pennsylvania's major products. Today, mining is only a small part of Pennsylvania's economy. However, eastern Pennsylvania produces almost all the country's anthracite coal. Anthracite is a hard type of coal that produces very high heat when it burns. Other mining products are limestone and natural gas.

▲ **One of Pennsylvania's chemical factories along the Allegheny River**

Chemicals are Pennsylvania's number-one factory product. They include medicines, paint, and chemicals made from petroleum (oil). Pennsylvania also produces computer parts and other electronics. The state is still a leading steelmaker, too.

Other factories make delicious things to eat—like chocolate! Milton Hershey built his first chocolate factory in 1903. Pennsylvanians also make cakes, cookies, pretzels, and ice cream. Is your mouth watering yet?

Milk is Pennsylvania's state beverage—and its leading farm product. Chickens, eggs, and beef cattle are among the state's other top products. Pennsylvania produces more mushrooms than any other state. Farmers there also grow corn and hay. Much of it ends up as cattle food.

▲ Hershey's factories can make more than 12 billion chocolate kisses each year.

About three of every four Pennsylvania workers have a service job. Some are bankers, teachers, hospital workers, or store clerks. Others work on computers or help tourists enjoy their visit. All of them use their skills to make life better for others.

▲ **A friendly park ranger at Raystown Lake State Park**

▲ These women are participating in the Million Woman March in Philadelphia against racism.

Who are Pennsylvanians? They are people of many **cultures.**
Most Pennsylvanians have European **ancestors.** They may
have come from Germany, Ireland, Italy, England, or Poland.
About one of every ten residents is African-American. People
of Asian and Hispanic cultures live in Pennsylvania, too.

Several groups of German people arrived in the 1600s and 1700s. They were seeking religious freedom. Their Amish and Mennonite religions were not welcome in Europe. Descendants of these people are called the Pennsylvania Dutch. That name comes from *Deutsch*, a German word meaning "German."

The Pennsylvania Dutch are sometimes called the "plain people." Their clothing is plain, and their lives are simple. They live in farming communities and use neither electricity nor cars. When any member is in need, the others pitch in to help.

▲ The Pennsylvania Dutch do their farming without modern equipment.

▲ Restaurants and shops in Philadelphia's historic Bourse Building

In 1770, Pennsylvania had the second-highest population among the colonies. Only Virginia had more people. Pennsylvania kept its number-two position until 1950. Today, it ranks sixth in population among all the states. The 2000 census counted more than 12 million Pennsylvanians. Philadelphia is the largest city. Next in size are Pittsburgh, Allentown, and Erie.

About one out of three Pennsylvanians lives in a rural area. These are areas in the countryside, away from cities. No other state has so many rural people.

Many beloved "stars" came from Pennsylvania. They include actors Bill Cosby, Jimmy Stewart, Grace Kelly, and W. C. Fields. The state's singers include Marian Anderson and Lena Horne. Author Louisa May Alcott was a Pennsylvanian, too. She wrote the classic children's books *Little Women* (1868) and *Little Men* (1871).

Pennsylvania also has its share of sports stars. Olympic skater Tara Lipinski was born in Pennsylvania. So were baseball player Reggie Jackson and golfer Arnold Palmer. Young baseball players get a chance to be stars in Williamsport. The Little League World Series is held there every August.

▲ **Comic Bill Cosby originally came from Pennsylvania.**

▲ **Champion ice skater Tara Lipinski won a gold medal at the 1998 Winter Olympics.**

▲ Philadelphia 76ers player Charles Barkley (left) was a member of the Pennsylvania basketball team for eight years.

The Philadelphia 76ers are the state's basketball stars. During baseball season, Pennsylvanians root for the Philadelphia Phillies and the Pittsburgh Pirates. Football season brings out fans of the Philadelphia Eagles and the Pittsburgh Steelers.

Punxsutawney is in the news every February 2. That's Groundhog Day. Everyone's watching a groundhog named Punxsutawney Phil. Will Phil see his shadow when he comes out of his burrow? If he sees his shadow, it is said that winter will last six more weeks. If he doesn't, spring is on its way!

▲ Each year when Phil comes out of his burrow, visitors watch to see if he casts a shadow.

▲ Life in Pennsylvania Dutch country is very similar to what it was like hundreds of years ago.

Girls stroll along in bonnets and long dresses. Boys in big-brimmed black hats glide by on old-fashioned scooters. Horse-drawn buggies rumble past on their way to market. Farmers guide mule-drawn plows across rolling fields.

Does this sound like an outdoor living-history museum? In a way, it is. It's Pennsylvania Dutch country in southeast Pennsylvania. There, people live as their ancestors did long ago.

Imagine how exciting it would be to create a new nation. You could make all your own rules! That's just how the United States began. It all happened in Philadelphia. There you can visit Independence Hall where the Declaration of Independence was signed. Nearby is Carpenters' Hall, where the First Continental Congress met.

▲ Philadelphia's Liberty Bell dates back to 1753. It was rung on important occasions, including the first reading of the Declaration of Independence in 1776.

Gettysburg National Military Park is near Pennsylvania's southern border. Thousands of graves honor the Civil War soldiers who died there. At the museum you'll see soldiers' uniforms and photos. You'll also see an old copy of Lincoln's Gettysburg Address.

▲ **Gettysburg National Military Park preserves the field where the famous battle took place.**

▲ **A view of the Pocono Mountains from Pickerel Lake**

Northeast Pennsylvania is perfect for nature lovers. They enjoy its forests, waterfalls, and clear mountain lakes. The Pocono Mountains and the Endless Mountains stretch on for miles. To the east, the Delaware Water Gap cuts a passage through the mountains.

In Harrisburg, you can tour the state capitol and its museum. If the general assembly is meeting, you're welcome to go in and watch.

Do you love chocolate? Then Hershey's Chocolate World is the place for you! Tour Hershey's factory, and you'll learn the secrets of making chocolate. Best of all, you'll get a tasty sample!

The Susquehanna River cuts a deep canyon near Williamsport. It's called the Grand Canyon of Pennsylvania. In town, the mansions of nineteenth-century millionaires

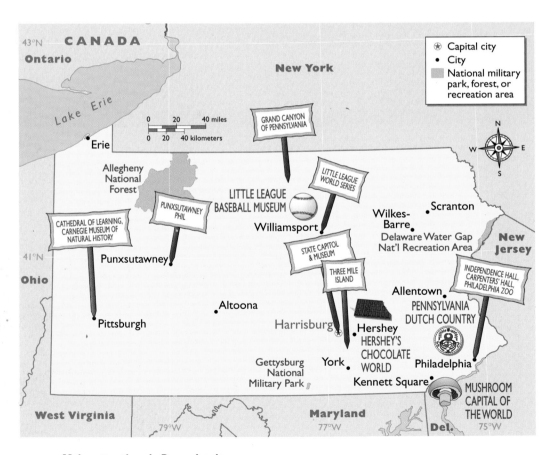

▲ **Major attractions in Pennsylvania**

line the streets. The Little League Baseball Museum is in Williamsport, too.

What are classrooms like in Africa, Israel, or Norway? You'll see them all in the Cathedral of Learning. That's a tower at Pittsburgh's Carnegie-Mellon University. Its twenty-four Nationality Classrooms celebrate the cultures of Pittsburgh's **ethnic** groups.

Put on your goggles and pick up your chisel. You're going on a dig for dinosaur fossils! You'll do it in Pittsburgh's Carnegie Museum of Natural History. This museum is famous for its dinosaur bones—and for its hands-on digging site.

▲ The Cathedral of Learning at Carnegie-Mellon University is at the heart of the campus.

Allegheny National Forest is north of Pittsburgh. Hiking through this wilderness, you'll see Pennsylvania as the Native Americans did. Move along quietly, and you'll see raccoons, beavers, and foxes. By then, you'll surely agree—Pennsylvania is a great place to explore!

▲ **Nature lovers enjoy the natural beauty of Allegheny National Forest.**

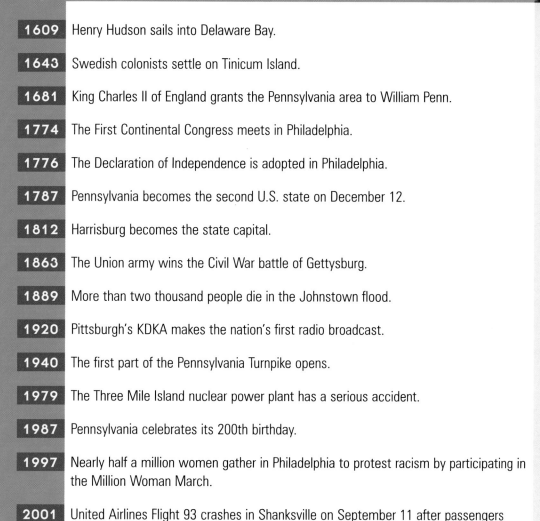

1609 Henry Hudson sails into Delaware Bay.

1643 Swedish colonists settle on Tinicum Island.

1681 King Charles II of England grants the Pennsylvania area to William Penn.

1774 The First Continental Congress meets in Philadelphia.

1776 The Declaration of Independence is adopted in Philadelphia.

1787 Pennsylvania becomes the second U.S. state on December 12.

1812 Harrisburg becomes the state capital.

1863 The Union army wins the Civil War battle of Gettysburg.

1889 More than two thousand people die in the Johnstown flood.

1920 Pittsburgh's KDKA makes the nation's first radio broadcast.

1940 The first part of the Pennsylvania Turnpike opens.

1979 The Three Mile Island nuclear power plant has a serious accident.

1987 Pennsylvania celebrates its 200th birthday.

1997 Nearly half a million women gather in Philadelphia to protest racism by participating in the Million Woman March.

2001 United Airlines Flight 93 crashes in Shanksville on September 11 after passengers confront terrorists who took control of the plane. It was one of four deadly attacks that day that killed thousands of people.

Glossary

ancestors—a person's grandparents, great-grandparents, and so on

colonists—people who settle a new land for their home country

colony—a territory that belongs to the country that settles it

constitution—the official rules about how a government is organized and works

cultures—groups of people who share beliefs, customs, and a way of life

economy—the way a government runs its industry and trades goods

electronics—devices that use tiny particles called electrons

ethnic—relating to a nationality or culture

fossils—forms left by ancient plants and animals

industries—businesses or trades

plateau—high, flat land

ridge—a sharp, rocky hill

tributaries—rivers that flow into a larger river

Did You Know?

★ The Hershey Company is the world's largest chocolate and cocoa maker.

★ Abraham Lincoln began his Gettysburg Address with, "Four score and seven years ago." He was referring to the country's beginnings. A score is twenty, so "four score and seven" is eighty-seven. Lincoln was speaking in 1863, and eighty-seven years earlier was 1776. That was the date of the Declaration of Independence.

★ Pittsburgh built the nation's first baseball stadium in 1909.

★ The first piano made in the United States was constructed in Philadelphia in 1775.

★ The nation's first daily newspaper was published in Philadelphia in 1784.

★ Pennsylvania is the only original colony that doesn't border the Atlantic Ocean.

★ Benjamin Franklin founded the Philadelphia Zoo. It was America's first public zoo.

★ Kennett Square is called the Mushroom Capital of the World.

State capital: Harrisburg

State motto: Virtue, Liberty, and Independence

State nickname: Keystone State

Statehood: December 12, 1787; second state

Area: 45,310 square miles (117,351 sq km); **rank:** thirty-third

Highest point: Mount Davis, 3,213 feet (979 m) above sea level

Lowest point: Sea level along the Delaware River

Highest recorded temperature: 111°F (44°C) at Phoenixville on July 10, 1936

Lowest recorded temperature: −42°F (−41°C) at Smethport on January 5, 1904

Average January temperature: 27°F (−3°C)

Average July temperature: 71°F (22°C)

Population in 2000: 12,281,054; **rank:** sixth

Largest cities in 2000: Philadelphia (1,517,560), Pittsburgh (334,563), Allentown (106,632), Erie (103,717)

Factory products: Chemicals, food products, electronic equipment

Farm products: Milk, chickens and eggs, mushrooms, beef cattle

Mining products: Coal, natural gas, limestone

State flag: Pennsylvania's state flag shows the state coat of arms. The background is blue, with gold fringe around the edges. The coat of arms is a shield with an American eagle on top. Two horses rear up

beside the shield. Within the shield are symbols of Pennsylvania's strengths. One is a ship, standing for trade. Another is a plow, representing natural resources. The three bundles of wheat stand for fertile fields. Beneath the shield are an olive branch and a cornstalk. They represent peace and plenty. At the bottom is a banner with the state motto: Virtue, Liberty, and Independence.

State seal: The state seal has the same symbols as the coat of arms. The main difference is that there are no horses. Lady Liberty is portrayed on the back of the seal— called the counter seal. Her foot stands on a lion. The lion represents tyranny, or unfair rule. Around the edge are the words, "Both Can't Survive." This means that people can have either liberty or tyranny.

State abbreviations: Pa. or Penn. (traditional); PA (postal)

State Symbols

State bird: Ruffed grouse

State flower: Mountain laurel

State tree: Hemlock

State animal: White-tailed deer

State dog: Great Dane

State fish: Brook trout

State insect: Firefly

State beverage: Milk

State beautification plant: Crown vetch

State ship: U.S. brig *Niagara*

State steam locomotive: K4s steam locomotive

State electric locomotive: GGI 4859 electric locomotive

State fossil: *Phacops rana* (a trilobite)

State commemorative quarter: Released on January 2, 2002

Making Pennsylvania Dutch Apple Crisp

The Pennsylvania Dutch often use fresh apples for cooking.

Makes six servings.

INGREDIENTS:

3 cups sliced apples

1 cup brown sugar

1/2 cup flour

1 teaspoon cinnamon

1/4 cup butter or margarine

1/3 cup chopped walnuts or other nuts

DIRECTIONS:

Make sure an adult helps you with cutting the apples and using the oven. Leave the butter or margarine out to soften. Preheat the oven to 375°F. Lay the apple slices in the bottom of an 8-inch-square baking dish. Mix the brown sugar, flour, cinnamon, and butter or margarine together. Using your hands, keep mixing until you have crumbly lumps. Mix in the nuts. Spread the mixture evenly over the apple slices. Bake 40 to 45 minutes. Apples should be softened and top should be light brown. Remove from oven and serve warm.

"Pennsylvania"

Words and music by Eddie Khoury and Ronnie Bonner

Pennsylvania, Pennsylvania,
Mighty is your name,
Steeped in glory and tradition,
Object of acclaim.
Where brave men fought the foe of freedom,
Tyranny decried,
'Til the bell of independence
Filled the countryside.

Chorus:
Pennsylvania, Pennsylvania,
May your future be
Filled with honor everlasting
As your history.

Pennsylvania, Pennsylvania,
Blessed by God's own hand,
Birthplace of a mighty nation,
Keystone of the land.
Where first our country's flag unfolded,
Freedom to proclaim,
May the voices of tomorrow
Glorify your name.

Famous Pennsylvanians

Louisa May Alcott (1832–1888) wrote *Little Women* (1868), *Little Men* (1871), and other books. They told about children growing up in the 1860s.

Marian Anderson (1897–1993) was an opera star. She was the first African-American to sing solo at New York's Metropolitan Opera.

James Buchanan (1791–1868) served as the fifteenth U.S. president (1857–1861).

Mary Cassatt (1844–1926) was a famous artist. Many of her paintings show mothers and their young children.

Bill Cosby (1937–) is one of America's most popular actors and comedians. Cosby (pictured above left) starred in "The Cosby Show," which ran for eight years on television.

W. C. Fields (1879–1946) was a motion-picture comedian. He usually played the part of a very grouchy man. His real name was William Claude Dukenfield.

Milton Hershey (1857–1945) opened the Hershey Chocolate Company in 1894. He gave most of his fortune to the Milton Hershey School for Disadvantaged Children.

Reggie Jackson (1946–) was a baseball player and a powerful home-run hitter. He was elected to the Baseball Hall of Fame in 1993.

Grace Kelly (1929–1982) was a motion-picture actress who became the princess of Monaco.

Tara Lipinski (1982–) is a champion ice skater. She won a gold medal at the 1998 Olympic Winter Games in Nagano, Japan.

George C. Marshall (1880–1959) was the U.S. Army chief of staff during World War II. After the war, he developed the Marshall Plan to help rebuild Europe. Marshall received the Nobel Peace Prize in 1953.

William McGuffey (1800–1873) was a schoolteacher and a minister. He wrote *McGuffey's Eclectic Readers* to teach children to read.

Lucretia Mott (1793–1880) was a leader for the women's rights and abolitionist movements in America.

William Penn (1644–1718) was the English Quaker who founded Pennsylvania. He believed in religious freedom and friendly relations with Native Americans.

Betsy Ross (1752–1836) was a seamstress. Many people believe that she made the first U.S. flag that had stars and stripes.

Andrew Wyeth (1917–) is a popular American artist. He paints people and places in Pennsylvania and elsewhere.

Want to Know More?

At the Library

Bartoletti, Susan Campbell. *Growing Up in Coal Country.* New York: Houghton Mifflin, 1996.

Italia, Bob. *The Pennsylvania Colony.* Edina, Minn.: Abdo Publishing, 2002.

Kroll, Steven, and Ronald Himler. *William Penn: Founder of Pennsylvania.* New York: Holiday House, 2000.

Osbourne, Mary Pope. *Standing in the Light: The Captive Diary of Catherine Carey Logan, Delaware Valley, Pennsylvania, 1763.* New York: Scholastic Trade, 1998.

Wellsbacher, Anne. *Pennsylvania.* Edina, Minn.: Abdo & Daughters, 1998.

Whitehurst, Susan. *The Colony of Pennsylvania.* New York: PowerKids Press, 2000.

On the Web

Discover Pennsylvania
http://sites.state.pa.us/kids/
To visit the state of Pennsylvania's kids' page, with a lot of facts and fun activities

Experience 100% Pure Pennsylvania
http://www.experiencepa.com
To see the state tourism site, with places to go and things to see and do

PA PowerPort
http://www.state.pa.us/PAPower/
To visit the state web site, with information on Pennsylvania's history, government, economy, and more

Through the Mail

Pennsylvania Department of Community and Economic Development
Center for Travel, Tourism and Film
Commonwealth Keystone Building
400 North Street, 4th Floor
Harrisburg, PA 17120
For information on travel, activities, and interesting sights in Pennsylvania

Pennsylvania Office of the Chief Clerk
Pennsylvania House of Representatives
Main Capitol Building
Harrisburg, PA 17120
For information about Pennsylvania's government and economy

Pennsylvania State Data Center
Penn State Harrisburg
777 W. Harrisburg Pike
Middletown, PA 17057
For Pennsylvania's facts and figures

On the Road

Pennsylvania State Capitol
Third Street between Walnut and North Streets
Harrisburg, PA 17120
800/868-7672

State Museum of Pennsylvania
Third and North Streets
Harrisburg, PA 17120
717/787-4978

Index

About the Author

Ann Heinrichs grew up in Fort Smith, Arkansas, and lives in Chicago. She is the author of more than eighty books for children and young adults on Asian, African, and U.S. history and culture. Ann has also written numerous newspaper, magazine, and encyclopedia articles. She is an award-winning martial artist, specializing in t'ai chi empty-hand and sword forms.

Ann has traveled widely throughout the United States, Africa, Asia, and the Middle East. In exploring each state for this series, she rediscovered the people, history, and resources that make this a great land, as well as the concerns we share with people around the world.